A Guidebook for Young People Studying US Slave Songs Part II

A Guidebook for Young People Studying US Slave Songs Part II

25 SECRET SACRED SONGS – DECODED

James Thomas and Lorna Andrade

Library of Congress Control Number: 2024904040
ISBN: Softcover   979-8-3694-1640-2
        eBook   979-8-3694-1641-9

Print information available on the last page.

Rev. date: 06/05/2024

To order additional copies of this book, contact:
Xlibris
844-714-8691
www.Xlibris.com
Orders@Xlibris.com
846935

To Alex Santos,
thank you for assisting with transcribing.

Contents

Dedication

This work is dedicated to the unknown slaves who used musical styles from Africa to communicate, escape, and survive slavery.

Many lives were lost pursuing freedom.

The Children's Questions Book #2

Spirituals

#1. "This Little Light of Mine": What Does It Mean to Have a Little Light That I Own?

#2. "Fare You Well": Where Are You Going?

#3. "I Want to Be Ready": What Do You Want to Be Ready For?

#4. "Swing Low": Are the People on a Swing and Is It Low?

#5. "Done, Made My Vow to the Lord": What Does It Mean to Make a Vow?

#6. "Every Time I Feel the Spirit How": How Do You Feel about the Spirit?

#7. "Wade in the Water": Are the Slaves in the Waters?

#8. "Didn't My Lord Deliver Daniel?": Who Is Daniel and Where Was He Delivered?

#9. "Steal Away": What Does This Mean to Steal Away?

#10. "Give Me Freedom": What Is Freedom?

#11. "Oh, Rise, Shine": Who Is Rise and Shine?

#12. "I Woke Up This Morning": Who Woke Me Up This Morning?

#13. "Wayfaring Stranger": What Does This Mean?

#14. "Welcome Table": Who Came to the Welcome Table?

#15. "In Bright Mansions": What Does This Mean?

#16. "Let Us Break Bread Together": Who Is the US Breaking the Bread?

#17. "There's a Meeting Here Tonight": Who Will Go to This Meeting and Why?

#18. "Don't Let Anybody Turn You Around": Who Is Trying to Turn Them Around?

#19. "My Lord, What a Morning": What Is Mourn In?

#20. "Gimme That Old-Time Religion": What Is an Example of Old-Time Religion?

#21. "Rock in Jerusalem": What Does This Mean?

#22. "Ride on King Jesus": Who is King Jesus and Where Is He Going?

#23. "There's No Hidden Place Down Here": Why Was There No Hidden Place Down There?

#24. "Climb Up the Mountain, Children": Did the Children Actually Climb Up the Ladders?

#25. "Dixie": What Is Dixie? Is It a Place?

Interviewed children by
Dr. Lorna Chambers-Andrade, Coauthor
A Guidebook for Young People Studying US Slave Songs. Winter 2023 yr.

Learning Objectives and Outcomes for Book 2

~Ongoing musical styles for communication is to touch your inner spirit by feeling the rhythm when hearing each word of the songs or musical instruments presented (decoding).

~Strength, each slave was soaring like on eagle's wings. They ran and did not grow weary; they walked and did not faint.

~The slaves let the light shine brighter, and darkness grow dimmer each day.

~Freedom from bondage, freed from fear, no more demeaning words, no more pain, sorrow, and mutilating deaths.

~You will further be able to assimilate with songs like the planting of seeds in soil for its strong roots to grow, and then begin to be selective with those stronger roots, thus the path to freedom as sang in song, digging deeper.

~Giant sign, a new level is coming for the freed slaves, going forward by faith with a strong constitutional attitude from the inherited roots born in each one of them.

~These are more quantitative results you will gain in the Guidebook #2 for Young People Studying US Slave Songs.

Bibliography and Footnotes References

Wikipedia Encyclopedia

The first slave song book was published in 1867 [1]

Origin songs sang in the fields, as work field holler, African music.

Spirituals: stem from the ring shouts, a circular dance to clapping and chanting was common among every plantation.

The slaves with spirituals had a social impact tied to the revolution of slavery eighteen sixty-five year.

Negro spirituals were among the first means of antiliteracy laws made it illegal for enslaved and free people of color to read or write. [2]

Black's keys were played by slaves they were not allowed/permitted to play white keys (example, "Amazing Grace").

The pentatonic scale lack keys played in sequence forms, a pentatonic scale note. [3]

Prior to the US Civil War, and emancipation spirituals were originally an oral tradition passed from one slave generation to the next. [4]

Biblical stories were memorized and translated into song. [5]

Following the emancipation, the lyrics of spirituals were now published. An example is the Fisk Jubilee Singers; established in 1871; popularized spirituals bringing it to wider international audiences. [6]

In 1920 Mamie Smith commercial was successful in starting a commercial recording industry, which increased audiences about spirituals. [7] 46

Black composers Harry Burleigh and R. Nathaniel Dett created a new repertoire for concert stages by applying their western classical education to the spirituals while the spirituals were created by a circumscribed community of people in bondages. Overtime, they were known as the first signatures in music in the United States. [8] 47

Spirituals were traced to Africa; Willian Francis Allen states: Spirituals regularly sung in America churches whose origins in plantations had not been acknowledged. He wrote it was almost impossible to convey the spirituals in print. Because of the inimitable quality of African American voices with its intonation as delicate variations where not one singer can be reproduced on paper, no two singers were identified as singing the same things. Then the lead singer started with words to be a verse, often improvising, and the chorus strikes in with refrains that, based on him, is called caller and response. [9]

Introduction

Anna Dukes was my great-grandmother on my father's side. She was born a slave in the late 1840s, we think. Few records were kept in those days, so we're not sure, but she was the first person to tell me about these songs. She referred to them as the secret sacred songs from the old days. Later in life when I went to Fisk University, I studied with John W. Work III. He was the director of the Fisk Jubilee singers and principally responsible for getting me in Fisk and inviting me to sing with the Jubilee singers.

The songs that I have chosen for this book are some of the examples of codes and messages that they contain. Some of the songs contain these codes, some complete songs are codes, and some songs don't have codes at all. I guess this intended to confuse those who don't believe that there were codes at all, which worked in the favor of the slaves. None of these songs had musical notes attached when they were created, and so in many cases, there are various versions to the same song. As the slaves were sold and sent from plantation to plantation, they would take these songs with them in their heads. Of course, there would be variations, and because this still exists, many critics refuse to believe that there were messages and codes at all.

And to the benefit of the slaves, many of the notes were not put on paper until after the Civil War.

Virginia Stone has produced illustrations.

Lorna Andrade developed young people's questions and learning objectives and bibliography research.

We collectively hope you enjoy this little book, Jim Thomas.

1. "This Little Light of Mine"–SOC*
2. "Fare You Well"–SOC
3. "I Want to Be Ready"–refrain SOC, verses call and response

4. "Swing Low"–refrain SOC, verses call and response
5. "Done, Made My Vow"–refrain SOC, verses call and response
6. "Every Time I Feel the Spirit–Syncopated
7. "Wade in the Water"–SOC
8. "Didn't My Lord Deliver Daniel?"–Refrain SOC, verses call and response
9. "Steal Away"–SOC
10. "Give Me Freedom"–SOC
11. "Oh, Rise, Shine"–refrain SOC, verses call and response
12. "I Woke Up This Morning"–refrain SOC, verses call and response
13. "Wayfaring Stranger"–SOC
14. "Welcome Table"– SOC
15. "In Bright Mansions"–SOC
16. "Let Us Break Bread Together"–SOC
17. "There's a Meeting Here Tonight"–SOC
18. "Don't You Let Nobody Turn You Around"–SOC
19. "My Lord, What a Mournin'"–SOC
20. "Gimme That Old-Time Religion"–SOC
21. "Rockin' Jerusalem"–refrain SOC, verses call and response
22. "Ride on King Jesus"–refrain SOC, verses call and response
23. "There's No Hidin' Place Down Here"–SOC
24. "Climbin' Up the Mountain, Children"–refrain SOC, verses call and response
25. "Dixie"–SOC

*SOC: slow opening cords.

The Three African Song Styles

Slow opening cords (SOC) means there is a gradual opening statement as presented in "This Little Light of Mine, I'm Gonna Let It Shine."

Syncopated indicates that the song begins one beat after the opening of the measure as in the spiritual "Every Time I Feel the Spirit."

Call and response describes an opening statement followed by a responding statement like "If you get there before I do"–the call–"Tell my friends I'm coming too"–the response.

#1
"This Little Light of Mine"

This song is a protest song. The slaves were told that they could not practice their religion from Africa, and they protested by creating this song "This Little Light of Mine. I'm Gonna Let It Shine." Sing it all day and go undetected as practicing their religion and protesting against what they had been told.

(Created by unknown slave)

This little light of mine
I'm gonna let it shine
This little light of mine
I'm gonna to let it shine
This little light of mine
I'm gonna to let it shine
Let it shine, let it shine, let it shine

Everywhere I go, I'm gonna let it shine
And everywhere I go, I'm gonna let it shine
Everywhere I go, I'm gonna let it shine
Let it shine, let it shine let it shine

All in my home, I'm gonna let it shine
All in my home, I'm gonna let it shine
All in my home, I'm gonna let it shine
Let it shine let it shine let it shine

#2
"Fare You Well"

    When the slaves were told which persons would be sold, they would conduct a little meeting at night in private; and those that were to be sold would go around in a circle, shaking everybody's hand and say, "Fare you well, fare you well. If I don't see you again, fair you well."

(Created by unknown slave)

Fare you well, fare you well, fare you well, everybody

Fare you well, fare you well, whenever I do get home

My sister said . . . Fare you well, etcetera

My brother said . . . Fare you well, etcetera

My mother said . . . Fare you well, etcetera

#3
"I Want to Be Ready"

    "I Want to Be Ready" is this song about Nat Turner and his insurrection. I want to be ready to walk in Jerusalem, just like John. John was the name given to Nat Turner, and Jerusalem is the name of the town where the insurrection took place.

(Created by unknown slave)

I want to be ready,
I want to be ready,
I want to be ready,
To walk in Jerusalem just like John

John said the city was just foursquare,
Walk in Jerusalem just like John.
And he declared he'd meet me there,
Walk in Jerusalem just like John

O John, O John, what do you say?
Walk in Jerusalem just like John.
That I'll be there at the coming day,
Walk in Jerusalem just like John

When Peter was preaching at Pentecost
Walk in Jerusalem just like John.
He was endowed with the Holy Ghost,
Walk in Jerusalem just like John

If you get there before I do,
Walk in Jerusalem just like John.
Tell all my friend I'm a-comin' too,
Walk in Jerusalem just like John.

#4
"Swing Low, Sweet Chariot"

This song is about the conductors on the underground railroad. When this song was sung, the conductors were nearby, waiting in the woods, to take the escapees on the underground railroad to freedom. The first verse is "I looked over Jordan and what did I see? A band of angels coming for to carry me home." *Angels* were conductors on the underground railroad.

(Created by unknown slave)

Refrain
Swing low, sweet chariot
Coming for to carry me home.
Swing low, sweet chariot,
Coming for to carry me home.

I looked over Jordan, and what did I see,
Coming for to carry me home.
A band of angels coming after me,
Coming for to carry me home.

If you get there before I do,
Coming for to carry me home.
Tell all my friends I'm coming too,
Coming for to carry me home.

I'm sometimes up and sometimes down,
Coming for to carry me home.
But still my soul feels heavenly bound,
Coming for to carry me home.

#5
"Done, Made My Vow to the Lord"

A most interesting song because the slaves were not allowed to make their own decisions, and so to make a vow to run away on the underground railroad was perhaps the very first time a slave made an independent decision. I will never turn back because it will compromise the underground railroad.

(Created by unknown slave)

Done made my vow to the Lord,
And I never will turn back,
I will go, I shall go to see what the end will be.

Sometimes I'm up, sometimes I'm down,
To see what the end will be.
But still my soul is heav'nly bound,
To see what the end will be.

I'll pray and pray and never stop.
To see . . .
Until I reach that mountain top.
To see . . .

#6
"Every Time I Feel the Spirit"

It's a song that seems just religion; however, if you look at the words to the first verse, "there ain't but one train runs on this track it runs to heaven," which is Canada, "and then right back" is where the code is. So every time I feel the spirit, it's not a religious song at all. It's a song that talks about the underground railroad

(Created by unknown slave)

Every time I feel the spirit
Movin' in my heart I will pray.
Yes, every time I feel the spirit
Movin' in my heart I will pray

There ain't but one train upon this track.
It runs to heaven and then right back.

#7
"Wade in the Water"

"Wade in the Water" was a song that is also a bit deceptive. It seems to be religious; however, Harriet Tubman taught the slaves that were escaping that "should you hear bloodhounds, the way to distract them and save your life is to wade in the water."

(Created by unknown slave)

Wade in the water
Wade in the water, children,
Wade in the water
God's a-going to trouble the water

Wade in the water
Wade in the water, children,
Wade in the water
God's a-going to trouble the water

Who's that young girl dressed in red
Wade in the water
Must be the children that Moses left
And God's gonna trouble the water

#8
"Didn't My Lord Deliver Daniel?"

This song brings up characters from the Old Testament of the King James Version of the Bible and states that if this western God could save these people in these horrible situations, then why can't he save me too? It's a song about universal justice. "Didn't my Lord Deliver Daniel? Then why not me as well?"

(Created by unknown slave)

Didn't my Lord deliver Daniel
Deliver Daniel, deliver Daniel?
Didn't my Lord deliver Daniel
And why not every man?

He delivered Daniel from the lion's den
Jonah from the belly of the whale
And the Hebrew children from the fiery furnace
And why not every man?

Didn't my Lord deliver Daniel
Deliver Daniel, deliver Daniel?
Didn't my Lord deliver Daniel
And why not every man?

#9
"Steal Away"

This song was created to be sung if the conductors for the underground railroad appeared during the day and they needed to get their escapees prepared. Then the workers around would sing, steal away, and one by one, those that were to escape would join the conductors in the woods nearby.

(Created by unknown slave)

Steal away, steal away
Steal away to Jesus
Steal away, steal away home
I ain't got long to stay here

My Lord, he calls me
He calls me by the thunder
The trumpet sounds within my soul
I ain't got long to stay here

#10
"Give Me Freedom (Jesus)"

This is an interesting song that was sung by the slaves who wanted nothing more than freedom. Freedom was so important to them; if they were singing that song and their owners walked into the room, they would simply change the word *freedom* to *Jesus*.

(Created by unknown slave)

In the morning, when I rise
In the morning, when I rise
In the morning, when I rise, give me freedom
(Jesus)

Give me freedom (Jesus)
Give me freedom (Jesus)
You can have all this world
But give me freedom (Jesus)

And when I am alone
Oh, and when I am alone
And when I am alone, give me freedom (Jesus)

Give me freedom (Jesus)
Give me freedom (Jesus)
You can have all this world
But give me freedom (Jesus)

And when I come to die
Oh, and when I come to die
And when I come to die, give me freedom (Jesus)

#11
"Oh, Rise, Shine"

"Oh, rise, shine for the lightest of coming." There's a song that was sung when they heard that the Union troops were coming to set them free. Oftentimes, without struggles, if they knew that the Union troops were nearby, they simply dropped their tools in the fields and walked away and would sing, "Oh, rise, shine for the light as are coming. My Lord said he's coming by and by."

(Created by unknown slave)

Oh, rise, shine! For the
light is a-comin',

My Lord says he's comin' by an' by.

This is the year of jubilee,
My Lord says he's comin' by an' by.
My Lord has set his people free,
My Lord says he's comin' by an' by.

Wet or dry, I intend to try,
My Lord . . .
To serve the Lord until I die,
My Lord . . .

I intend to shout an' never stop,
My Lord . . .
Until I reach that mountaintop,
My Lord . . .

#12
"I Woke Up This Morning"

"I woke up this morning with my mind and it stayed, stayed on freedom." Freedom again? Yes. It's what the slaves desired, and they could sing all day that they woke up with their mind fixed on Jesus or some other thing; but it was really always freedom

(Created by unknown slave)

I woke up this mornin'
with my mind, stayin' on
freedom
Woke up this mornin'
with my mind, stayin' on
the freedom
Well, woke up this
mornin' with my mind,
stayin' on freedom

Hallelu, hallelujah, hallelujah

Singin' and prayin' with my mind stayin' on,
freedom
Singin' and prayin' with my mind stayin' on the
freedom
Singin' and prayin' with my mind stayin' on,
freedom
Hallelujah, hallelu, hallelujah

Well, I'm walkin' and talkin' with my mind stayin'
on freedom
Walkin' and talkin' with my mind stayin' on the
freedom
Well, walkin' and talkin' with my mind stayin' on
freedom
Hallelujah, hallelu, hallelujah

#13
"Wayfaring Stranger"

The slaves always wanted people to know that this was not their original home and that they were here as wayfaring strangers, but one day they had a home over Jordan and they would get there by and by. "I am a poor, wayfaring stranger in this land."

(Created by unknown slave)

I am a poor wayfaring
stranger
Traveling through this
world of woe
There is no sickness, toil,
or danger
In that fair land to which
I go

I'm goin' home to see my
mother
I'm goin' home, no more
to roam
I'm just goin' over
Jordan
I'm just goin' over home

#14
"Welcome Table"

"Welcome Table." The slaves were servants and always served meals at the welcome table where they knew they were not welcome, and so they would sing about a time when they could sit at the welcome table and there would be no manners. There would be all types of people. They could do what they wanted to do and enjoy themselves too. We're gonna sit at the welcome table one of these days.

(Created by unknown slave)

I'm gonna sit at the
welcome table
I'm gonna sit at the
welcome table one of
these days, hallelujah
I'm gonna sit at the
welcome table
Sit at the welcome table
one of these days, one
of these days

No fancy style at the
welcome table

No fancy style at the
welcome table one of
these days, hallelujah

No fancy style at the
welcome table

I'm gonna sit at the welcome table, hallelujah

All kind people at the welcome table . . .

#15
"In Bright Mansions"

    "In Bright Mansions" is really about life after death. That would give the slaves an opportunity to live in those wonderful homes that they could not live in on Earth, but after death, they would live in bright mansions above.

(Created by unknown slave)

In bright mansions
above
Lord, I wan' t' live up
yonder
In bright mansions
above

My mother's gone to
glory
I wan' t' go there too
Lord, I wan' t' live up
yonder
In bright mansions
above

My father's gone

My sister's gone . . .

My brother's gone . . .

My Savior's gone . . .

#16
"Let Us Break Bread Together"

"Let us break bread together on our knees" is an interesting little song because it just tells them turn to the east and watch the sunrise facing the east. Of course, you're facing Africa.

Let us break bread together on our knees.

(Created by unknown slave)

Let us break bread
together on our knees
Let us break bread
together on our knees
When I fall on my knees,
with my face to the rising
sun
Oh Lord, have mercy on
me

Let us drink wine
together on our knees
"repeat"

Let us praise God together on our knees
"repeat"

Oh Lord, have mercy on me
"repeat"
Lord, have mercy on me
"repeat"

#17
"There's a Meeting Here Tonight"

"There's a meeting here tonight." This is an announcement song. When they knew that they were going to have a little prayer meeting or they little get together or preparation for the escapees for the underground railroad, they would sing and this is one of the songs that would announce the meeting and they would just sing about fires in the east and the west and that would tell them where to go and which group was meeting.

(Created by unknown slave)

Get you ready . . . there's
a meeting here tonight
Come along there's a
meeting here tonight

I know you by your daily
walk there's a meeting
here tonight

Camp meeting in the
wilderness there's a
meeting here tonight

I know it's among the
Methodist there's a
meeting here tonight

My father says it is the
best to live and die a
Methodist there's a meeting here tonight

There's fire in the east, there's fire in the west
there's a meeting here tonight

I know it's among the Methodist there's a
meeting here tonight

Get ready . . .

#18
"Don't You Let Anybody Turn You Around"

"Don't You Let Anybody Turn You Around" is an interesting song used a lot during the civil rights movement during the 1960s. But actually, the song is a joke. That is the only one of these songs, among all of these songs that I consider a joke. For an example in the first verse, baptism was born in the Jordan. It was born in the Jordan River. And John baptized. A many person, but he sprinkled not A1. A joke, all of the verses of this song are jokes.

(Created by unknown slave)

Don't you let anybody
turn you around,
Turn you around, turn you
around;
Don't you let anybody
turn you around,
Keep the straight and
the narrow way

It was at the river of
Jordan baptism was
begun, John baptized the
multitude but he
sprinkled nary one

The baptism they go by
water. The Methodist go
by land but when they
get to heaven, they'll
shake other's hand

You may be a good
baptism and a good
Methodist as well but if you ain't the pure in heart
Your soul is bound for hell

#19
"My Lord, What a Mournin'"

"My Lord, what a mournin'." A mournin' was a gutteral sound made in the back of the throat. And it describes a sound that is made in a religious meeting when the slaves were really enjoying themselves moaning. It was a sound and when they state that when they state did . . . um . . . on judgment day that would be a great moaning. It was not morning as in good morning; it was a moaning. My Lord, what a moaning. When the stars begin to fall . . .

(Created by unknown slave)

My Lord, what a
mournin'! My Lord, what
a mournin'! O my Lord,
what a mournin'! When
the stars begin to fall.

You'll hear a sinner
mourn, to wake the
nation's underground,
Looking to my God's
right hand, when the
stars begin to fall.

You'll hear a sinner
pray, to wake the
nation's underground,
Looking to my God's
right hand, when the
stars begin to fall.

#20
"Gimme That Old-Time Religion"

"Give me that old time religion. Give me that old time religion. Give me that old time religion. It's good enough for me." Sounds simple enough, doesn't it? But if they could have been talking about the religions of Africa, give that to them and that is good enough.

(Created by unknown slave)

Give me that old-time
religion

Give me that old-time
religion

Give me that old-time
religion

It is good enough for me

It was good for my
mother

It was good for my
father

It was good for my
mother

It is good enough for my . . .

#21
"Rockin' Jerusalem"

 "Rockin' Jerusalem." "Rockin' Jerusalem" includes Mary and Martha, whose names, I think, were euphemisms in order to protect an actual character. So Mary and Martha will always be rocking Jerusalem. It's another song about Nat Turner's insurrection. Rocking Jerusalem . . . Jerusalem is where the insurrection took place.

(Created by unknown slave)

Oh Mary, o Martha
Oh Mary, o Martha
Oh Mary, gon' ring them
bells

I hear archangels
rockin' in Jerusalem
Hear archangels ringin'
them bells
Hear archangels rockin'
in Jerusalem
Hear archangels ringin'
them bells
Church gettin' higher
(Rockin' in Jerusalem)
Church gettin' higher
(Ringin' them bells)
Church gettin' higher
(Rockin' in Jerusalem)
Church gettin' higher
(Ringing them bells)
Oh Mary, o Martha
Oh Mary's gonna ring
them bells
Oh Mary, o Martha
Oh Mary's gonna ring
them bells

Hear archangels rockin' in Jerusalem
Hear archangels ringing them bells
Hear archangels rockin' in Jerusalem
Hear archangels ringing them bells
New Jerusalem, New Jerusalem
Gon' ring them bells
I hear archangels rockin' in Jerusalem
Hear archangels ringing them bells
Hear archangels rockin' in Jerusalem
Hear archangels ringing them bells
Them bells!

#22
"Ride on King Jesus"

 "Ride on King Jesus." To the slave, King Jesus was anybody who protected and supported the slave. That person was King Jesus to them, and so it was confusing to some people to hear right on King Jesus thinking that they were talking about a religious character, when in fact anyone who was supporting them was considered King Jesus

(Created by unknown slave)

Oooh ride on King
Jesus, ride on
No man no can a hinder
thee

Ride on King Jesus, ride
on
No man no can a hinder
thee

King Jesus ride on a
milk white horse

No man no can a hinder
thee

The river Jordan He did
cross

No man no can a hinder
thee

Ride on King Jesus, ride
on
No man no can a hinder
thee

#23
"There's No Hidin' Place Down Here"

There is no hiding place down here. The slave owners and drivers were able to engage some of the slaves as to tell them what was going on, or if there were insurrections planned, or whatever. And the other slaves did not like these people who were snitching on them. And so they would finally determine who it was that was telling these things and disappear them. And then they would sing to each other. There's no hiding place down here. They would refer to those folks as sinners and so forth and they were horrible. They were horrible, but they would, they would disappear them and say "Well, there's no hiding place."

(Created by unknown slave)

There's no hiding place
down here
There's no hiding place
down here
I ran to the rock just to
hide my face
And the rocks cried out,
no hiding place
There's no hiding place
down here

There's no hiding place
down here
There's no hiding place
down here

The Devil wears a
hypocrite's shoe
And if you don't watch
out he'll slip it on you
There's no hiding place
down here

#24
"Climbin' Up the Mountain, Children"

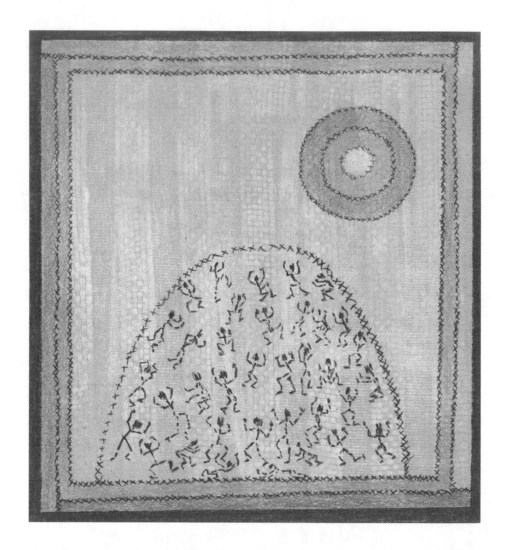

"Climbing Up the Mountain, Children." Another song that tells everybody, "this is not my home. I'm just not here just for this day, so I'm just climbing up this mountain doing what I have to do now. But after a while, I'll be gone." And they mentioned some of the characters from the Old Testament again and how they were spared by the great spirit; and they are thinking that this is going to happen to me as well, but at the moment, I'm just climbing up the mountain. Not here before this day.

(Created by unknown slave)

Climbing up the
Mountain, children
(Oh Lord I) Didn't come
here for to stay
(Oh Lord) If I never more
see you again
Goin' to meet you at the
judgement day

Climbing up the
mountain children
(Oh Lord I) Didn't come
here for to stay
(Oh Lord) If I never more
see you again
Goin' to meet you at the
judgment day

Hebrew in de fiery
furnace and dey begin
to pray and de good
Lawd smote dat fire out
Oh, wasn't dat a mighty
day! Good Lord, wasn't
dat a mighty day!

Daniel went in de lions
den and he begin to
pray and de angels of
de Lawd locked de lions
jaw Oh, wasn't dat a
mighty day! Good Lord,
wasn't dat a mighty day!

Climbing up the
Mountain, children

#25
"Dixie"

    This song was created by two brothers who were former slaves, Dan and Lou Snowden, who taught it to Dan Emmett. Emmett included it in his New York City minstrel show where it became an immediate hit in 1859.

(Created by unknown slave)

I wish I was in the land
of cotton
Old times, they're are
not forgotten
Look away, look away,
look away, Dixie Land

In Dixie Land where I
was born in
Early on one frosty
morning
Look away, look away,
look away, Dixie Land

Oh, I wish I was in Dixie,
away, away
'Cause in Dixie Land, I'll
take my stand
To live and die in Dixie
Away (away), away
(away), away down
south in Dixie

Jim Thomas, directing some members for choir
Note: Mostly white members here!

Bibliography

Gates, Henry Louis, Jr. Edited with Introd., *The Classic Slave Narratives*, New American Library: 1987.

Kilbrideon, Dan, Audio: 59:12, Discussion with an American Scholar re: culture, History, Sparks, Randy J., *Where the Negroes Are Masters*, Harvard University Press 2014, January 1, 2015.

"Oral History is very difficult to interpret and while a story may contain obvious errors, that does not mean it can be summarily dismissed," pg. 12.

Srinivas Aravamudan, 1999, *Tropicopolitans: Colonialism and Agency*, 1688–1804, Duke University Press. 251. IBN 978-08223-2315-0.

Sparks, J. Randy, *Where the Negroes Are Masters*, pgs: 14, 16 46, 47, 48, ibid., Harvard Press: November 18, 2013.

The Commission Bicentennial of United States Constitution, [The Constitution of United States and with Index Declaration of Independence, Washington DC. Sixth Ed. 1988 and Eighteen with Twenty Seventh Amendment Ed. 1992, Amendment XIII Ratified December 6, 1865], pg. 25, OP CIT.

The Process of Enslavement at Anamaboe, movement of slave route. pg. 131, ibid.

Wiencek, Henry, 2003, *An Imperfect God: George Washington, His Slaves, and the Creation of America*, first. Ed., Farrar, Straus, and Giroux, New York.

Wortman, Marc, *Secrets of American History, True Colors, Smithsonian*, October 2014, vol. 45, #6.

References

Allen, William Frances, Charles Pickard Ware, and Lucy Kim Garrison. *Slave Songs in the United States*. New York: A Simpson & Co, 1867.

Boatner, Edward. *The Story of the Spirituals*. Miami: Belwin Mills, 1973.

Dett, R. Nathaniel. *Religious Folk Songs of the Negro* as sung at Hampton Institute. Hampton, VA: Hampton Institute, 1927.

Dixon, Crista. *Negro Spirituals: From Bible to Folksong.* Philadelphia: Fortress Press, 1976.

Epstein, Dena J. *Sinful Tunes and Spirituals: Black Folk Music to the Civil War.* Chicago: University of Illinois Press, 1977.

Johnson, James Weldon, and J. Rosamond Johnson. *American Negro Spirituals*. New York: DaCapo Press, 1923: reprint, New York. Viking Press, 1969.

Biographies: Jim and Lorna and Virginia

Jim Thomas, Founder of US Slave Song Project Spirituals Choir

Jim Thomas was born in Humboldt, Tennessee, in 1939. He attended Fisk University in Nashville, Tennessee, where he studied history and government and earned a BA degree. While at Fisk, Jim was invited to sing with the world-renowned Fisk Jubilee Singers. Later he sang with Robert Shaw Chorale in Atlanta, Georgia, and the Paul Hill Chorale at the John F. Kennedy Center for the Performing Arts in Washington, DC.

He founded and was the director of the Red Cross Festival Choir. They performed from 1976 to 1999.

He received awards: in 2000, Red Cross President's Leadership Award, and in 1999, American Red Cross-National Diversity.

Jim held numerous leadership positions within the American Red Cross and special assignments for the IRCE, which included service at military installations in Vietnam and Germany and special assignments in Austria and Sweden for youth leadership. He was a team leader for MASH director assignment to Jordan and served as a team leader in Liberia and Malawi for Friendship Africa. At NHQ in Washington

DC, he served as director of program development and corporate planning. Prior to early retirement, Jim spent his last seven years in role of corporate EEO, which included responsibility for Minority initiatives. He has worked for and been affiliated with the Red Cross for sixty years. Jim has served on the Red Cross board of directors for Fredericksburg, Virginia, and Hyannis Massachusetts.

The US Slave Song Project Inc., a nonprofit 501c3 organization, was founded by James E. Thomas in 2005 and is dedicated to educating the public about the history and interpretation of authentic US Slave Songs through presentations and performances. Jim serves as president of the choir director for US Slave Song Choir and narrates events and presentations.

From 2005 to 2007 Jim served as the cofounding director of the Martha's Vineyard Branch NAACP Spirituals Choir.

Lorna E. Chambers-Andrade, Educator
RN, BSN, MEd, MBA-PhD

Lorna a retired professor in professional nursing education, premedical and gerontology, and health administration and management.

She remains active with guest lectures and consulting at notable institutions of higher education and community health centers. She sits on many boards, contribute to public speaking, a lobbyist, and an author and workshop designer on issues, ranging in strategies we can use for reducing violence in black communities to management of health care facilities with a special focus on adult day care facilities in rural areas, such as on Martha's Vineyard. Her master's thesis, "Opening Up an Adult Day Health Care Facility in a Rural Setting, Cambridge College, August 1986," is used by many rural areas even today!

She is a member of numerous professional organizations, and she is listed in Who's Who in American Universities, Who's Who in Nursing, and Who's Who of Women Executives, and in Fourth Edition International Biographical Center Cambridge, England, Men and Women of Distinction. She is also a research fellow by American Biographical Institute 2006.

At the present, she continues to lobby for the rights of rural areas in regions to have access to local public higher education facilities. She continues to fundraise for scholarships.

She is a former vice president of Martha's Vineyard Local Chapter of the NAACP and presently a board member. She cofounded the Martha's Vineyard Spiritual Choir, with Mr. James Thomas.

She is a member of the US Slave song Project Spiritual Choir, which has a mission and vision to educate the masses on slavery with songs and history presentations.

She loves to sing and loves studying black history through lyrics and song with a special interest on the evolution of slavery.

Virginia Fishburne Stone, Illustrator

She has a master's degree in painting from Cranbrook Academy of Arts Bloomfield Hills, Michigan, and a bachelor's degree in studio art from University North Carolina, Chapel Hill North Carolina. She also studied figure drawing under Seminar for College Teachers at New York University in Anthropology Department of NYU where she studied African systems of thought under T. Biederman.

Virginia sings in Jim Thomas's the US Slave Song Project USA Choir, with Dr. Lorna Chambers-Andrade.

Printed in the United States
by Baker & Taylor Publisher Services